Houses

Harley Chan

I live in a place that is very hot.

2

People here build houses
with clay.
Clay keeps houses cool inside.

4

5

I live in a place where it snows a lot.

7

People here build houses with strong, steep roofs.
The snow slides off the steep roofs.

I live in a place where it rains a lot.

10

People here build houses on stilts.
Heavy rain can cause floods.
Stilts keep the houses above
the water.

12

13

I live in a place where it is very rocky.
It is windy here, too.

People here build houses into the rocks.
The rocks protect the houses from the wind.